The TODDLER'S handbOOK

with over **100 Words**
that every kid should know

BY DAYNA MARTIN

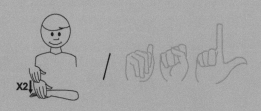

ENGAGE BOOKS

VANCOUVER

1

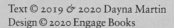 

Mailing address
PO BOX 4608
Main Station Terminal
349 West Georgia Street
Vancouver, BC
Canada, V6B 4A1

www.engagebooks.com

Written & compiled by: Dayna Martin
Edited & translated by: A.R. Roumanis
Illustrations by: Julian Rodriguez
Proofread by: Katherine Velliquette
Designed by: A.R. Roumanis
Photos supplied by: Shutterstock

LIBRARY AND ARCHIVES CANADA CATALOGUING IN PUBLICATION

Title: The toddler's handbook : with over 100 words that every kid should know /
by Dayna Martin.

Names: Martin, Dayna, 1983–, author

Description: Text in English and illustrated American Sign Language.

Identifiers: Canadiana (print) 20190143525 | Canadiana (ebook) 20190143584
ISBN 978-1-77226-629-0 (hardcover). –
ISBN 978-1-77226-628-3 (softcover). –
ISBN 978-1-77226-630-6 (pdf). –
ISBN 978-1-77226-631-3 (epub). –
ISBN 978-1-77226-632-0 (kindle)

Subjects:
LCSH: American Sign Language – Vocabulary – Juvenile literature.
LCSH: Vocabulary – Juvenile literature.
LCSH: Word recognition – Juvenile literature.

Classification: LCC HV2476.4 .M37 2019 | DDC J419/.7081 – DC23

ABCs 4

NUMBERS 11

MANNERS 14

COLORS 16

OPPOSITES 18

SHAPES 24

ACTIONS 28

EMOTIONS 30

SPORTS 32

ENGINES 34

SIZES 36

BODY 38

DISHES 40

CLOTHES 42

BATH 44

BED 45

3

Apple

Bus

Crayons

Dinosaur

4

Elbow
Ee

Fish
Ff

Grapes
Gg

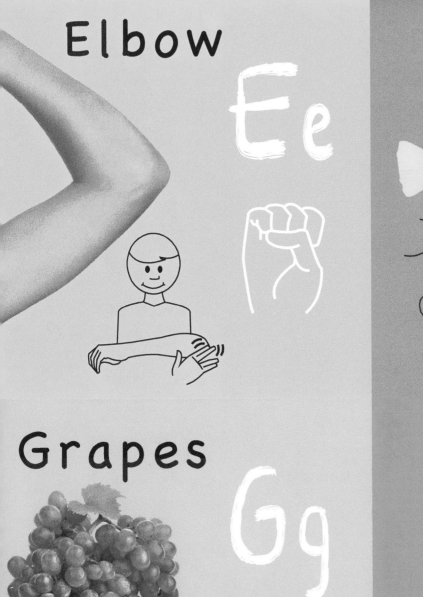

House
Hh

5

Ice cream

Ii

Jacket

Jj

Kite

Kk

6

Ladder

Milk

Net

Orange

L l

M m

X2

N n

O o

X2

7

Pizza

P p

Queen

Q q

Robot

R r

8

Scissors

S s

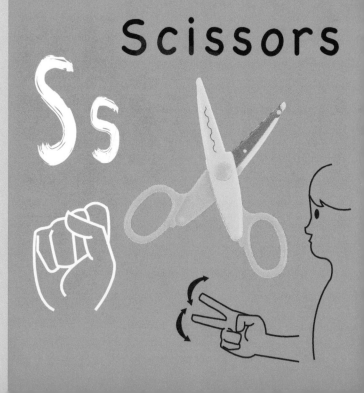

Tape

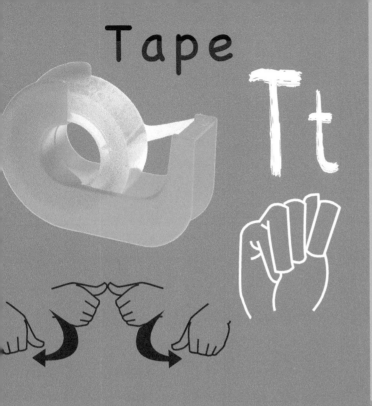

Umbrella

Vacuum

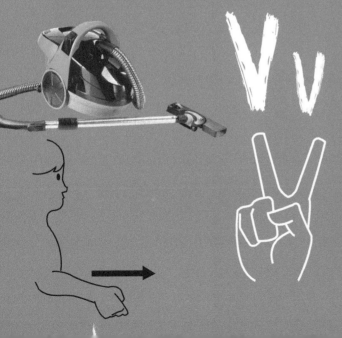

Wheelchair

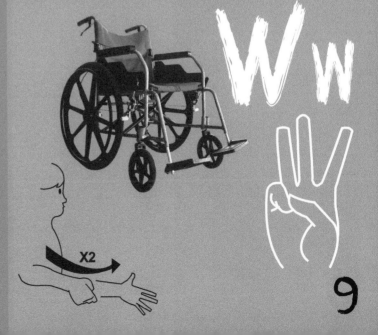

9

Xylophone

Xx

Yogurt

Yy

Zipper

Zz

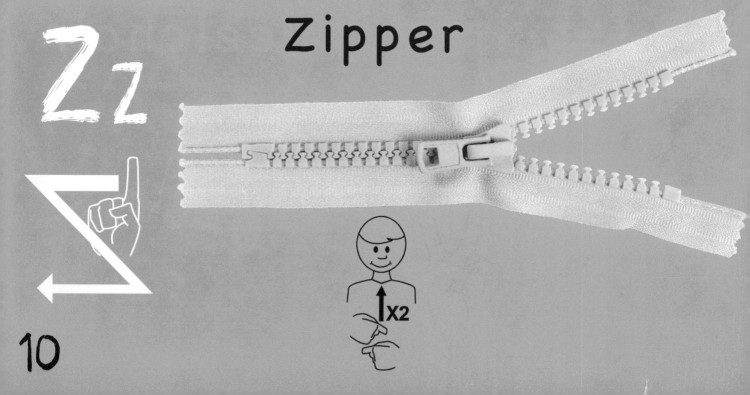

Sandwich

One
1

Crackers

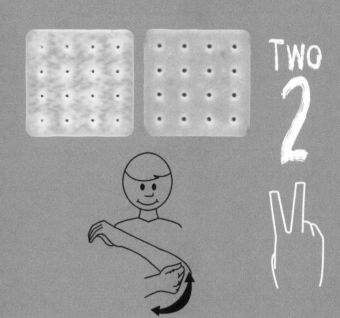

Two
2

Bananas

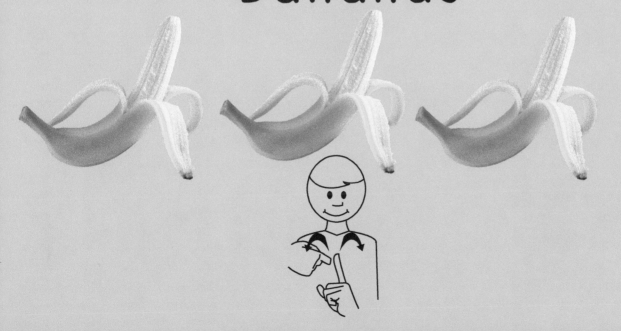

Three
3

11

Strawberries

Four

4

Carrots

Five

5

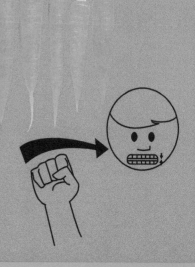

Tomatoes

Six

6

12

Pumpkins

Seven

7

Cherries

Eight

8

Potatoes

Nine

9

Cookies

Ten

10

Good morning

Hello

14 Please

Thank You

Goodbye

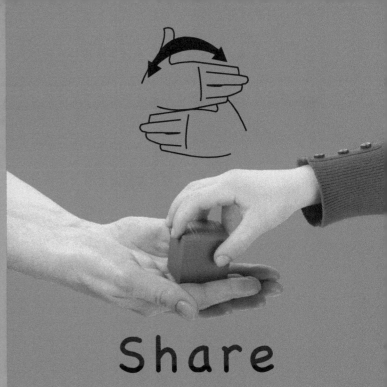

Share

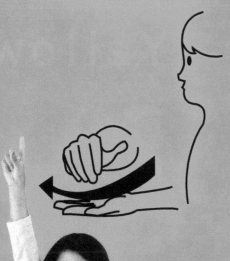

Excuse me

Good
night

15

Rainbow

Red

Orange

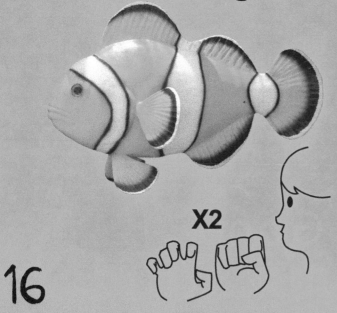

X2

16

Yellow

Green

Blue

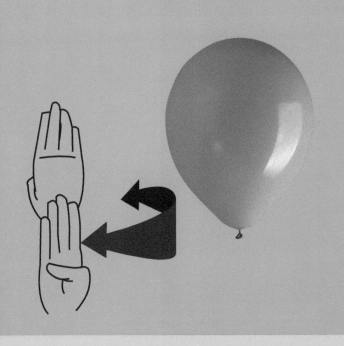

Purple

Pink

X2

17

Up

Down

In

Out

18

Hot

Cold

Wet

Dry

19

Front

Back

On

Off

20

Open

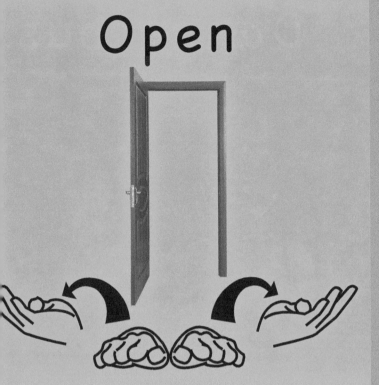

Closed

Empty

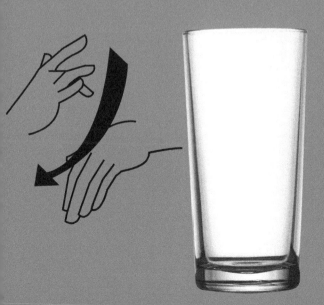

Full

21

Safe

Dangerous

Fast

Slow

22

Asleep

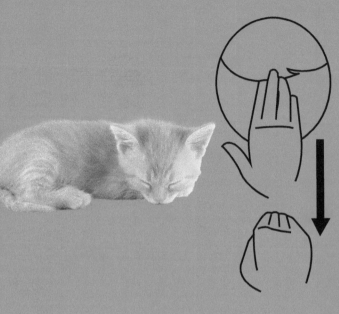

Awake

Sit

Stand

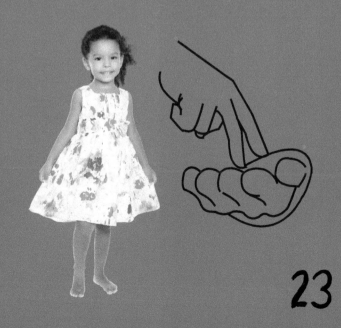

23

Circle

Square

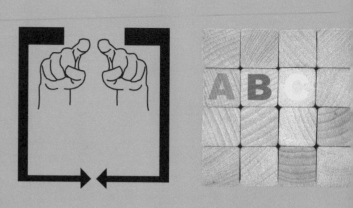

Triangle

Rectangle

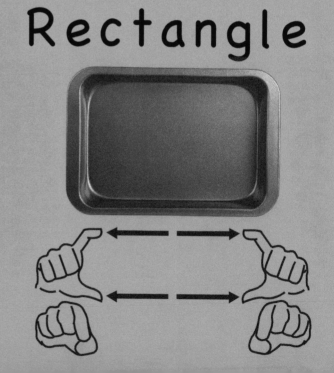

24

Diamond

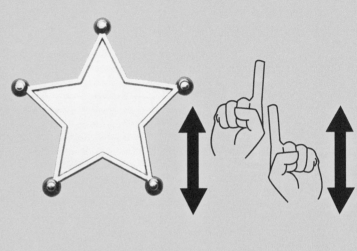

Star

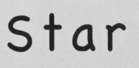

Oval

Heart

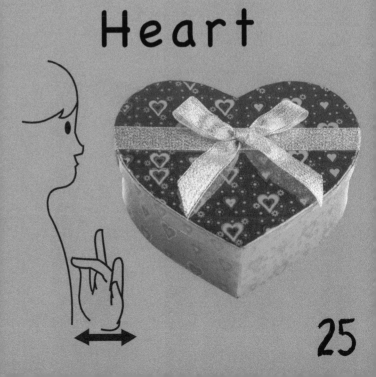

25

Sneeze

Clap

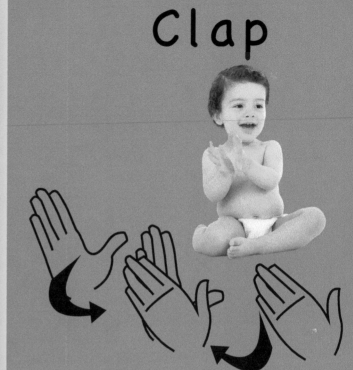

Hush

26

Ring

Breakfast

Snack

Lunch

Dinner

27

Crawl

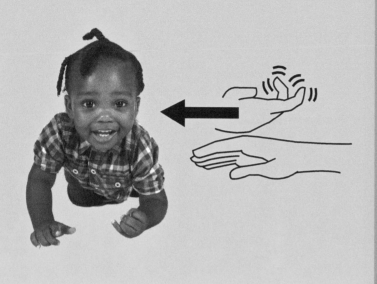

Roll

Walk

Run

28

Hop

Ride

Kiss

Jump

29

Happy

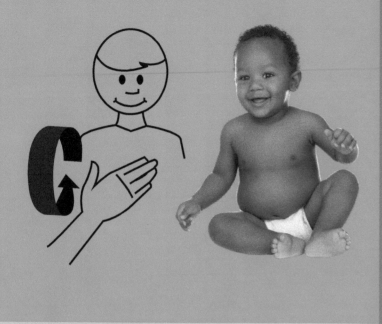

Sad

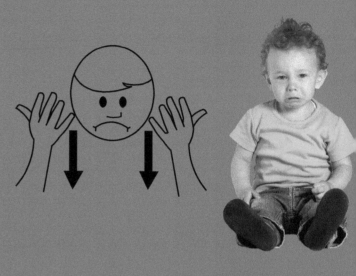

Angry

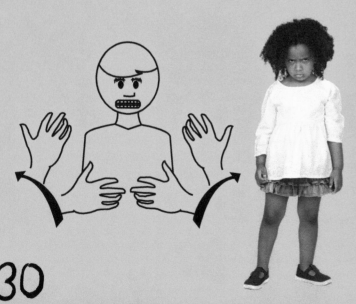

Scared

30

Frustration

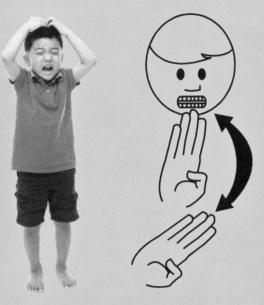

Surprise

Shock

Brave

31

Baseball

Basketball

Tennis

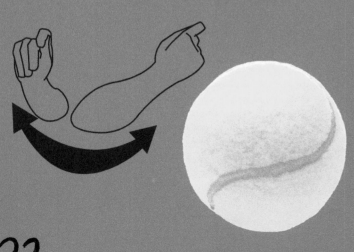

Soccer

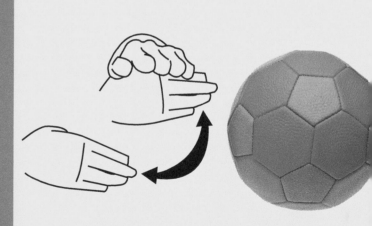

Badminton

Football

Volleyball

Golf

33

Fire truck

Ambulance

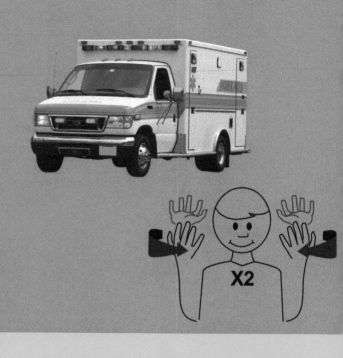

Car

Police car

34

Helicopter

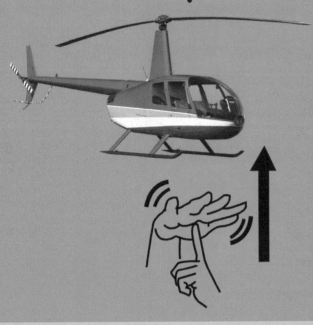

Airplane

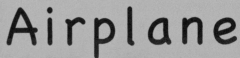
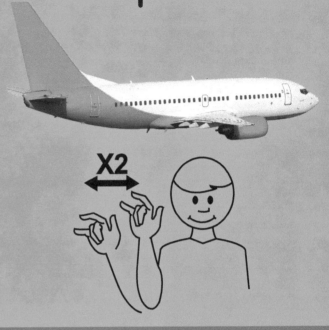

Train

Boat

Flowers

Small

Medium

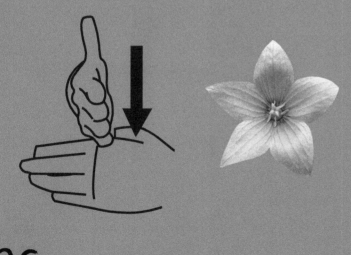

Large

36

Slide

Playground

Teeter toter

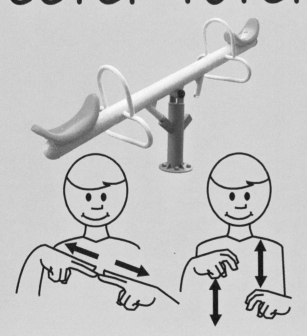

Swing

37

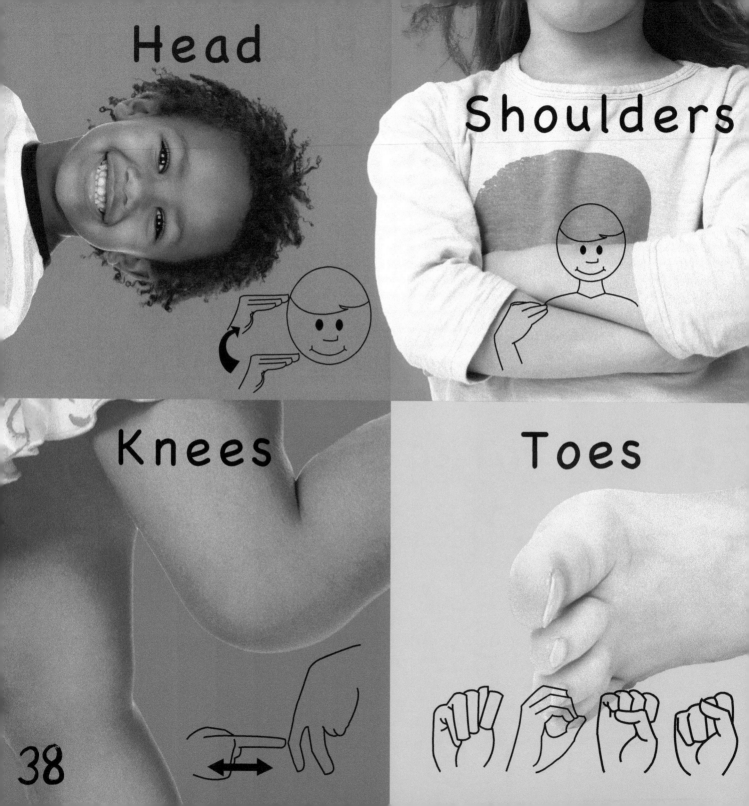

Head

Shoulders

Knees

Toes

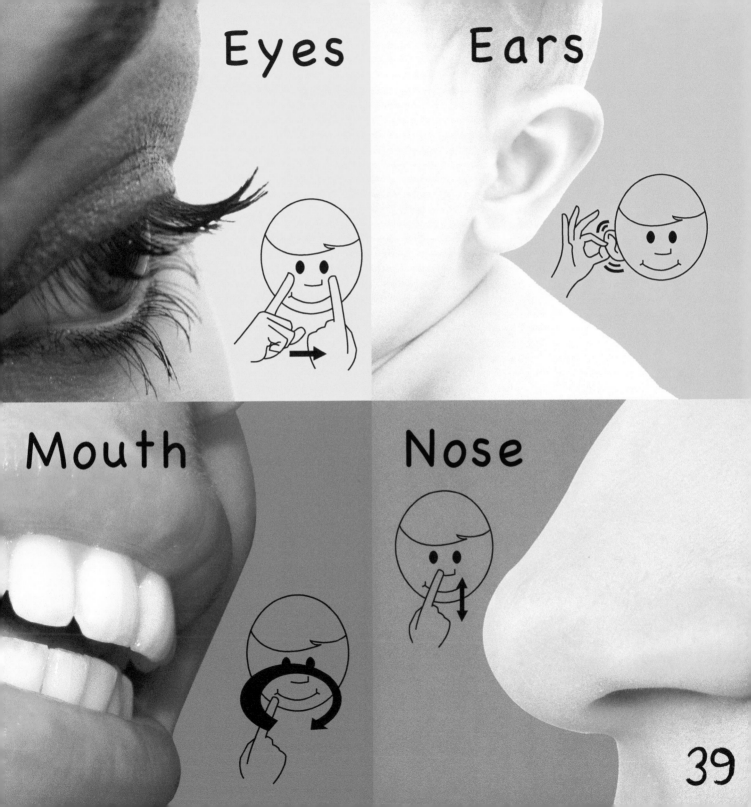

Eyes

Ears

Mouth

Nose

39

Mug

Bowl

Pot

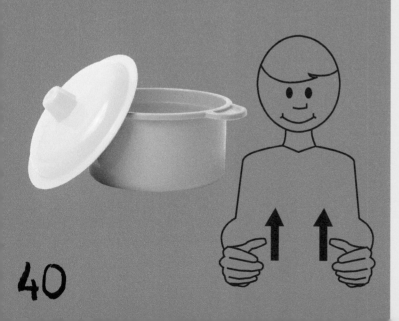

Cup

40

Plate

Fork

Knife

Spoon

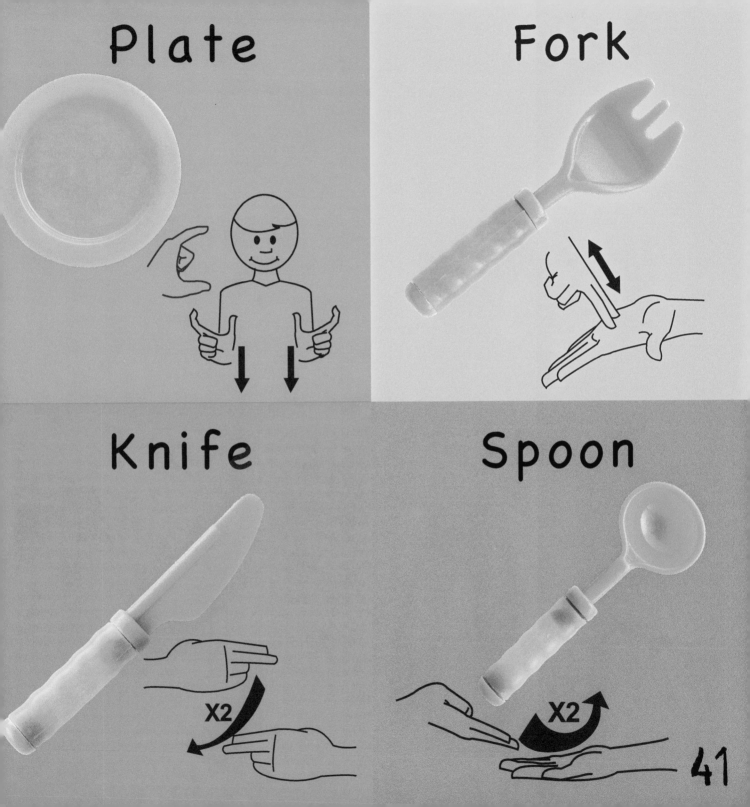

41

Hat

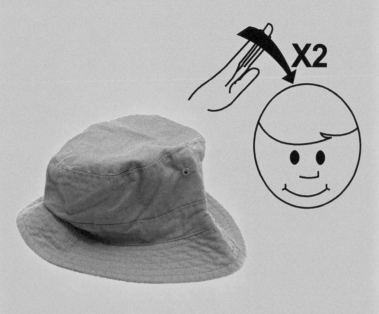

Shirt

Pants

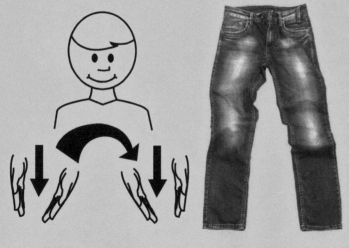

Shorts

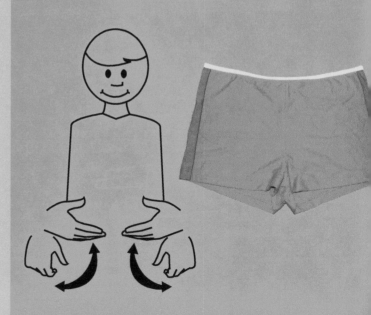

42

Gloves

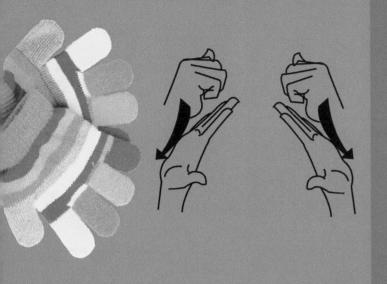

Sunglasses

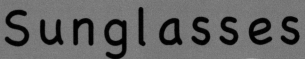

Socks

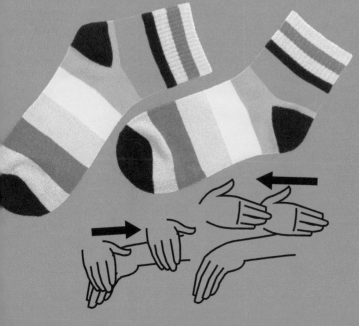

Shoes

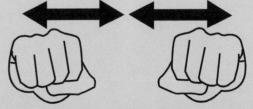

Bath

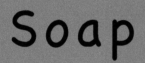

Soap

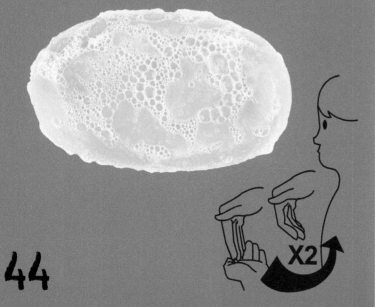

Towel

44

Toothbrush

Book

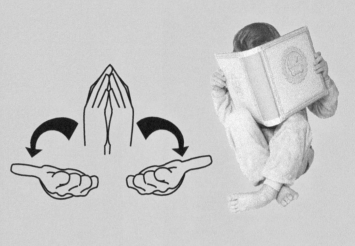

Potty

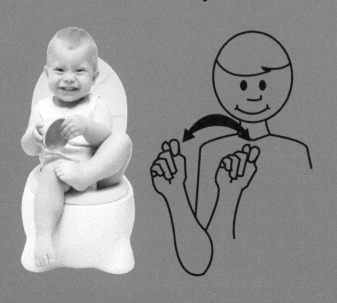

Bed

45

THE T♡ddlER'S handbOOk

Match the following to the pictures below. Can you find **7 pumpkins, a dinosaur, a rainbow, a baseball, a lion, a square, a sad boy, a helicopter, and shoes?**

activity /

helicopter /

shoes /

orange /

baseball /

7 pumpkins /

sad /

46 dinosaur /

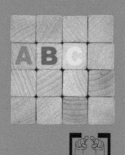

square /

rainbow /

ENGAGING READERS — LEVEL 1 READING TOGETHER
The Solar System
Ashley Lee — EXPLORING SPACE

ENGAGING READERS — LEVEL 1 READING TOGETHER
Birds
ANIMALS
Ashley Lee

ENGAGING READERS — LEVEL 2 READING WITH HELP
Frogs
ANIMALS
Ashley Lee

ENGAGING READERS — LEVEL 2 READING WITH HELP
Plastics
EARTH
Ashley Lee

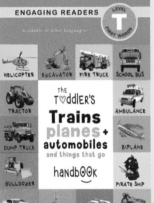

ENGAGING READERS — LEVEL T FIRST WORDS
The Toddler's Trains planes + automobiles and things that go handbook
HELICOPTER, EXCAVATOR, FIRE TRUCK, SCHOOL BUS, TRACTOR, AMBULANCE, DUMP TRUCK, BIPLANE, BULLDOZER, PIRATE SHIP, MUSCLE CAR, TUG BOAT, POLICE CAR, TRAIN

ENGAGING READERS — LEVEL T FIRST WORDS
The Toddler's handbook
With over 100 Words that every kid should know
NUMBERS, COLORS, SHAPES, ABCs, OPPOSITES, SIZES, FOOD, ENGINES, SOUNDS, TIME, ACTIONS, SPORTS, BODY, EMOTIONS

ENGAGING READERS — LEVEL P EARLY CONCEPTS
The Preschooler's handbook
With over 300 Words that every kid should know
ABCs, NUMBERS, COLORS, SHAPES, MUSIC, SCHOOL, MANNERS, MATCHING, BIKING, GARDENING, JOBS, ARTS, BRUSH TEETH, POTTY

ENGAGING READERS — LEVEL K READY FOR SCHOOL
The Kindergartener's handbook
With over 300 Words that every kid should know
ABCs, COLORS, MATH, SHAPES, VOWELS, TIME, SEASONS, SENSES, WEATHER, RHYMES, CALENDAR, PATTERNS, SCHOOL, CHORES

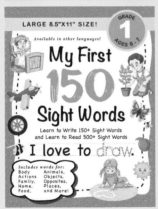

LARGE 8.5"X11" SIZE! — GRADE 1 AGES 6-7
Available in other languages!
My First 150 Sight Words
Learn to Write 150+ Sight Words and Learn to Read 500+ Sight Words
I love to draw.
Includes words for: Body, Actions, Family, Home, Food, Animals, Objects, Opposites, Places, and More!

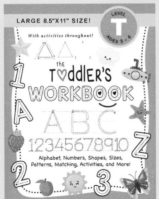

LARGE 8.5"X11" SIZE! — LEVEL T AGES 3-4
With activities throughout!
The Toddler's WORKBOOK
ABC 12345678910
Alphabet, Numbers, Shapes, Sizes, Patterns, Matching, Activities, and More!

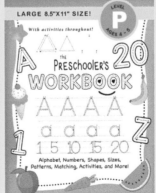

LARGE 8.5"X11" SIZE! — LEVEL P AGES 4-5
With activities throughout!
The Preschooler's WORKBOOK
A 20 a 1 5 10 15 20
Alphabet, Numbers, Shapes, Sizes, Patterns, Matching, Activities, and More!

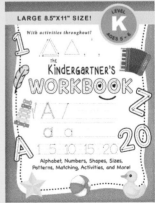

LARGE 8.5"X11" SIZE! — LEVEL K AGES 5-6
With activities throughout!
The Kindergartner's WORKBOOK
d a 1 5 10 15 20
Alphabet, Numbers, Shapes, Sizes, Patterns, Matching, Activities, and More!

Have comments or suggestions?
Contact us at: alexis@engagebooks.ca

 Show us how you enjoy your #engagingreaders. Tweet a picture to @engagebooks for a chance to win free prizes.

CPSIA information can be obtained
at www.ICGtesting.com
Printed in the USA
LVHW071735150621
690284LV00006B/342